Tightrope

Selina Tusitala Marsh

AUCKLAND
UNIVERSITY
PRESS

First published 2017
Reprinted 2017, 2018, 2019

Auckland University Press
University of Auckland
Private Bag 92019
Auckland 1142
New Zealand
www.press.auckland.ac.nz

ISBN 978 1 86940 872 5

A catalogue record for this book is available from
the National Library of New Zealand

Book design by Katrina Duncan
Cover design by Spencer Levine

Printed in China by Everbest Printing Investment Ltd

Tightrope

for

Teresia Teaiwa
shooting black star
(1968–2017)

Contents

I   ABYSS

The Dogs of Talimatau   3

Apostles   7

Alice's Chickens   12

Led by Line   13

The Blacking Out of *Pouliuli* (1977)   14

Tantrum Tightrope   22

Kiwitea Street in the '80s   24

Le Coup   25

The dark ground   27

gafatele   28

Siren   29

Discover the question   31

Explanation of Poetry to My Immigrant Mother   32

II   TIGHTROPE

Unity   37

!   39

Pussy Cat   41

Queens I have met   42

Out of one mountain   47

Dinner with the King   48

Whispers and Vanities   50

Burning hands   51

Inwood Hill, New York   52

Before making war   53

Insurance Broker-Turned-Counsellor-Playwright, Rumba Café   54

When others glare　56

Subway Lingo from 190th to 42nd Street　57

Sicilian-Hungarian-Jersey-born Tape-Artist, Union City　58

The *New York Times*, April 21 2015　61

The story began　62

Eviction Notice 113　63

Essential Oils for the Dying　65

Bread Bags　68

Atoll Haiku Chain　69

Alofa the only　70

Nadadola Road　71

Apia Seawall　73

The genesis of the world　74

Path　75

III　TRICK

Believe in the plot　79

The Working Mother's Guide to Reading Seventy Books a Year　80

Be afraid of nothing　82

Like the Time You Were Four　83

Orange Crayon Stick Figure Man　85

Marriage　87

Belief in Jack Kerouac　90

Lies sometimes　92

Red Comb　93

Black White Desiring　94

In Creative Writing Class　95

Warrior Poetry　96

Never wound　99

Ka'ena: Leaping Point　100

We are what we remember, the self is a trick of memory . . .
history is the remembered tightrope that stretches across
the abyss of all that we have forgotten.
– MAUALAIVAO ALBERT WENDT

I

abyss

The Dogs of Talimatau

(for Uncle Siva)

My son finds a tail
on the lawn
a paw on the drive
a snapped-off jaw
round the back
by the washing line.

The night before
in heat we'd heard
Max V, Lima and Ono
(knotted fur, nettling bones
fat eyes, fat hunger)
snapping, snarling.

In the morning
we open the back door
parting sooty
veils of flies
to find
a hind leg, half a head
the bloated innards
of another dog.

However that dog died
(probably on the road)
however long ago
(at least two days)
Max V, Lima and Ono

sniffed out its decayed meat
dragged it home
and in pecking order
began to eat.

Lords of Pouliuli.

Hot stench
makes us gag
slamming the door
on the buzzing swarm
we yell for Uncle
who dons his navy
blue work overalls
grabs a spade
Don't worry, I take it.
Good, bury it deep, we think.

We watch through blinds
as Uncle divides the black sea
scoops up head, carcass, tendon-threaded leg
and standing by the neighbour's fence
hefts the lot
over.

You know,
in old time
the high chief
they eat
the enemy
Max V, Lima and Ono
they like the high chief.

In Niu Sila
Uncle had one dog for years – Max,
then in Samoa three dogs
all named Max
who died
one by one
mysteriously.

The three preceding Maxes
were poisoned
according to Uncle
staring at the neighbour's fale.
After Max IV
finished foaming at the mouth, convulsing
Uncle went to think out loud
in front of the neighbour's house.

You know,
dogs are like the people.
They have thinking like the people
feeling like the people
spirit like the people.
I know God love the dogs.
I know that if this happen again
He will strike down
not the mans who do
this terrible thing
but the grandchildren
of the mans
because that is what the dogs
like to me – grandchildren.
Anyway,
have a good day, a ea?

Max V, Lima and Ono
lie in the shade
of the cookhouse
eating papaya skin, banana peel
soured koko Samoa
left-over two-minute beef noodles
but their favourite
according to Uncle
is the one tala bread
from Farmer Joe's.
Uncle's so proud
of the smartness of his dogs
one loaf lasts them
the whole week.

Apostles

Alice Walker said
before placing a red
cushion in the middle of the road
that poetry is revolutionary.

Sometimes I don't believe her

even though
I'm writing about Pacific apostles
twelve disciples of the Word
the first twelve women poets mostly as yet unheard

they are lava
they are mother
they are urohs and eros
they are flying fish out of water.

See,
I was googling 'betel nut: PNG'
a mild narcotic, like kava
wrapped in daga leaf
the nut is chewed with crushed
coral and shell
well, that makes lime
alters the pH levels
in your mouth
turning saliva scarlet
hence the bloody splotches
on Port Moresby's streets, bins, seats
windows, benches, signs, cars, shop-front ledges

before the total ban
in January this year.
I'm not a chewer myself but my husband tried it
a Solomon Island student
offered it
a sign of hospitality
of friendship
beer and betel nuts for all
even his teeth pinking
after chewing chewing.

I was googling
about acid in the mouth
oral cancers and ulcers.

I was googling
about lime, its burning
and up comes a photo.

A brown woman is sitting
her back to us
bare on a corrugated
iron dock
noose round her neck
wrists bound
machete bites
mar her back
one gash so deep
its creviced meat
blackens
in the smoking air.

I cannot see her face

but the encircling crowd can
three-year-old boy leaning on the young man can
little girl in the red polka-dot skirt holding her father's hand can too
gangs of youths stoke the irons
in the open barrel.

I cannot see her face

but Sister held back by policeman can
policeman held back by the mob can
fire-truck driver blocked by the mob can, too.

Her shoulders have lost
their angular protest
and hang askew
her skin is silent.

The behaviour of a witch
if ever they saw one
the highland bush sings

the trial begins.

Blogs tell me
many tried to stop
the staking, the poker burning.
I am told
her seventy-year-old mother struggled to free her
they broke her pelvis, her femur.

Sister cannot comprehend
how both crawled their way
through dirt and mob

to the church back door step
flesh burning between daughter's legs
soldered by soldiers against sorcery.

Mother and daughter are taken
into custody
for their own protection.
Police made attackers sign
a promissory note
to leave them alone.

Sister never sees them again.

But there is no doubt
as to the whereabouts
of twenty-year-old mother of two
Kepari Leniata
blamed for the
unexplained death
of a six-year-old boy.

Dragged from her hut
strung up
like a pig
she bore the dance of knives and burning rods
four hours
before being staked on an unholy altar

piles of used Huggies nappies
Marengo miscellanea and tyres
black-red with spit

then lit.

This mob are more sophisticated
mining-money orientated
armed cell phones
and steady hands
posting pics on instagram.

Not in the '40s of Jackson's 'Lottery'
but in February, 2013.

Alice, how can poetry possibly
revolutionise?

Kepari Leniata
Kepari Leniata
Kepari Leniata
Kepari Leniata
Kepari Leniata
Kepari Leniata
Kepari Leniata
Kepari Leniata
Kepari Leniata
Kepari Leniata
Kepari Leniata
Kepari Leniata

Alice's Chickens

pock in the yard of universal truths
peck at the glory of the earth
pluck fat grubs from under land's skin
these chickens are the life they hold within

Alice, on her green
meditation stool
coos to her red
combed miracles

Led by Line

(for Oceania's poetry foremothers)

We are led by line

blood line   love line   land line

     the stitched line
        is a fine line
           when out of line
             with the colonial line

we are led by line

horizon line   body line   fault line   fissure line

        is out of line
           with the imperial line
             the buried-head-in-the-sand line

we are led by line

lining up   our spoken lines   broken lines

     lines of disintegrating harmonies
        when we realign
           laying it on the line
             by drawing our line in the sand

The Blacking Out of *Pouliuli* (1977)

Al,
I've taken a black vivid marker
pressed it against your page
and letter by space by word by phrase
inked across your lines
streaking pouliuli pathways
wending in and out of the Void

Al,
the black ink on black font cracks open lines with lava tracks that
frack the land of your story hijack meaning ransack intention back-
packing on your own invention hacking into wise-cracking about
the side-tracking and bric-a-brac-ing of lines till back-to-back black-
on-black makes the night's page shoot stars lighting up windows of
words where we peer into pouliuli.

pouliuli

black out poems

wake up

Samoa   and brings

a

New Zealand

storyteller

A PEN

Books   , Road,

Books   worth,
          sex,
     Books,
New
     Books   wood,

Books   Street,

Books
Wendt

without   prior   permission

with

sadistic curiosity

pain

will eat your

protest

the

uncivilised

own nothing but

defiant breath
honest

chores;

and

the edge of

a

lavalava

3

the darkness,

loves

a sleepless night.

a

returning

hive of
strings too tightly tuned

stories

cure the incurable

Tantrum Tightrope

after watching him stare down eternity
sink guppy-gulping soundlessly

after seeing a filming glaze
become a second reptilian eye
snaking its way over

his blue-earthed orbs
the inhale
is stopped mid-way

by his soul
that slippery thing
fleeing to somewhere other

than this body, this bed
this hospital room
this building, this street, this world

I watch the fitting of
the death mask
involuntary, embarrassing, ugly

his face squirms
under its infinite grip

eeling tongue slips the pool
of his mouth
thickens, angles south

jaw stiffens straining north
pulling his face
tightrope taut

– you'd miss it
if you weren't nose to nose –
the tantruming body

unyielding before dying
a Hieronymus
come to life

as my father
lies unreturned
before me

Kiwitea Street in the '80s

Gran's jasmine
delicate pink

heavy and sweet
clings to the bone

wild green
loquat bell jars

plum magazines
splayed across

turtle neck blades
as the shadow alphabet

begins to play on
her cherry biscuit tin

a ball of wool
a white mohair kitten.

Le Coup

When I was three
and breaking the law
by placing one foot
in front
of the other
never looking down
or back
just straight ahead
on the seven-foot
pool fence
in Avondale

in New York
Philippe Petit
was breaking the law
placing one foot
in front
of the other
never looking down
or back
1,350 feet
above the earth
between the Twin
Towers ambulating
back and forth
eight times
as the world held
its breath
for the death
defying art

criminal
one week shy
of 25.

Philippe, flexing
along the petite wire
tongues the air
chews humidity
tasting to see
if rain is
there or
not there
a cloudburst
would wash
away his life
illegal alien
illicit street
juggler tossing
about in the mists
air choreographer
winds back
inertia and time
not a circus
tent in sight
just curtains
of art and opera
rising, the theatre
of poetry
beginning
as Philippe
scores
the line.

the dark ground,

whole passages.   recited

bone by bone

to

identify

the brutal
memory   root

gafatele

(for Rooney)

bloodgirl lived in a sleepy how town
(with up all few bird words down)
bloodgirl scrubbed her skin with their bones
carbon, dirt, diamond, stone

sleepy how town frowned, locked her far
bloodgirl congealed, slipped through the bars
painted her why on all whose doors
carbon, fire, glass, ore

gafatele drew his many hows down
(with flying whys and who shoulds around)
gafatele marked exs, crossed noughts
crystal, ruby, sardonyx, quartz

questions inked (both big and small)
bloodgirl and gafatele faced the wall
scribed their hows, etched their mights
alum, galena, bismuthinite

Siren

Mother's name is Sailigi
Samoan for siren

Born in Apia
September '44
On the night
The sirens
Mother
Daughter
Screamed

One year after Olaf Frederick Nelson died
One year before American Allies
Dropped atomic bombs on Hiroshima

Diamond ring on her hand
Passport in the other
Two decades later
She leaves for Niu Sila

Dad waits in Avondale
With my three Māori half brothers
He failed to mention them
To my 21-year-old mother
(in Emilio's Bar on Beach Road, Apia)

On Avondale Road
Evacuation soon began
As the first of many sirens rang
Leaving me and my sister
In the emptying house to sing

We won the war
In 1944
Because 1945
Did not rhyme.

discover   the

question   recognise

How

to follow

Explanation of Poetry to My Immigrant Mother

(for Glenn)

Ma, Ma, sometimes a
a poem's like
the Dawn Raids
2am door pounding
blue-uniformed belligerence
checking under beds
in closets
for illegal rhythms
overstaying rhymes

even cupboards are cleared for evidence
an extra pair of adjectives
might give away
the real number of lines
living in this poem.

Or Ma, a poem's like learning English
from Stefano DiMera and Marlena
as their *Days* become our *Days*
like sands through the hourglass
language staged
in click of tongue, cock of brow.

Or like when Selwyn Toogood
yells *Is It The Money Or The Bag?*
and the poem
every time

chooses the bag –
metaphorically speaking.

Or the poem's like the flea-market
at Avondale Racecourse
car boot mouths gaping
orange paisley silk
ochre itchy wool
slung over the side
waiting to be inhaled
by the wind's throat.

Or Ma, Ma, the poem's like the kids' lucky dip bin
love, grief, rage wrapped in headlines
bow tied with rippling alliteration
guesses up for grabs.

Or Ma, a poem's like one of those government schemes
set up by Paddy Walker in the '50s
someone had wrapped wood
in the *Sunday News* and lit
a fire in the oven
so they ran classes
about how to set the poem's knobs
how to ignite its hob
how the poem's mouth
begins to roast the day's meat.

Or how the poem
is a passport
can transit the likeness of you
from New Lynn

to Niutao
fending off heat and mosquitoes
how its sound and image, its push and pull
can launch you across lined waters
where in another country
you find yourself
home.

II

tightrope

Unity

(written and performed for Her Majesty Queen Elizabeth II,
Westminster Abbey, 2016)

Maluna aʻe o nā lāhui apau ke ola ke kanaka
'Above all nations is humanity' – Huwaiian proverb

Let's talk about unity
here in London's Westminster Abbey

did you know there's a London in Kiritimati?
Republic of Kiribati, Pacific Sea.

We're connected by currents of humanity
alliances, allegiances, histories

for the salt in the sea, like the salt in our blood
like the dust of our bones, our final return to mud

means though 53 flags fly for our countries
they're stitched from the fabric of our unity

it's called the Va in Samoan philosophy
what *you* do, affects me

what *we* do, affects the sea
land, wildlife – take the honeybee

nature's model of unity
pollinating from flower to seed

bees thrive in hives keeping their queen
unity keeps them alive, keeps them buzzing

they're key to our fruit and vege supplies
but parasitic attacks and pesticides

threaten the bee, then you, then me
it's all connected – that's unity.

There's a 'U' and an 'I' in unity
costs the earth and yet it's free.

My grandad's from Tuvalu and to be specific
it's plop bang in the middle of the South Pacific

the smallest of our 53 Commonwealth nations
the largest in terms of reading vast constellations

my ancestors were guided by sky and sea trails
and way before Columbus even hoisted his sails!

What we leave behind matters to those who go before
we face the future with our backs, sailing shore to shore

for we're earning and saving for our common wealth
a common strong body, a common good health

for the salt in the sea, like the salt in our blood
like the dust of our bones, our final return to mud

means saving the ocean, saving the bee
means London in the UK seeing Ronton in the South Seas
and sharing our thoughts over a cuppa tea

for there's a 'U' and an 'I' in unity
costs the earth and yet it's free.

!

*(a back-translation of 'Unità', translated
into Italian by Francesca Benocci)*

When I quit kneeling by the Western abacus
New Zealand became obedient in story
percolating the sale of air and crying
come sail the sanguine sea!

Come, laugh, pulverise delicatessens
of cheeses, mangoes and estranged lovers
just be sure never to fia sio in Samoa
its charismatic volcanoes

will see-saw swing to your talking ear
its mountains and fountains shape
domestic scenes leaping prosperously
into the verb village valley, vast and regal.

We'll unite the mountains in winter, villagers said
keep the mountains in rotation
so they channel nostalgic
reservoirs of verdant fruit

may attention to pesticides and parasites
not prime us for the sun's cold pit
they understand everything in the college
of eco-united – it costs magnificent gratitude.

My no one in Tuvalu
adds essence to mulato

fabrications lying
on atolls of pacification.

Pews in the church of Oceania
have maggots, termites. In letters of constellations
the mewling of cheaters combine aches and pens
they are molten prime numbers anchored

with passionate stares quell your lascivious
diet of colour and vengeance, the rest
a guardian to all universal schisms
vanquishing coast after coast.

Respond to me, nuzzle and come closer
for you commune with corpses of saints
who dance robust perfumed salsas
over the stage in comfort zones

that pulverise and ossify mangoes
and seagulls, these signify the salvation
of the ocean, the salvation
of domestic spaces.

If you read nothing, you love nothing.
Your charred remains
will linger suboceania
my beloved, my condemned rose acid

it will cost you Mondays
and gratitude.

Pussy Cat

Pussy cat, pussy cat
Where have you been?
I've been to London to visit the Queen.

Pussy cat, pussy cat
What did you there?
I frightened the Western world with my big hair.

My moana blue Mena
My Plantation House shawl
My paua orb
My Niu Ziland drawl
My siva Samoa hands
My blood red lips
My Va philosophising
My poetic brown hips
Then standing before Her Majesty
And the Duke of Edinburgh
I centred Polynesian navigation
Making sure to be poetically thorough
In proposing a timeline
Inverting West is Best
Instead drawing a circle
Encompassing all the rest.

Queens I have met

Dr Ngahuia

You wear royalty
on your chin
moko kauae
marks spirit kin of another queen
Te Arikinui Dame Te Ātairangikaahu
hawk of the morning sky
the longest glide
over Taupiri mountain
an unmarked grave framed
by Tyrian purple roses.
Your crowning hair
now spiky and short
is flecked by degrees
an MA on Frame
a PhD on Te Arawa
your people, Tūhoe, Waikato
your black leather robe flows
your Westminster is made
from Aotearoa clay
your rituals
vestibules of karakia
story, scholarship
lit in hollow alcoves
of stone, bone, flesh
Queen Tahuri.

HRH Elizabeth II

Nine decades
of blue linen rule
the longest ever
we were both born
on April 21st
you in '26
me in '71
when we meet
kanohi ki te kanohi
I am exactly half your age
and for a second
think to mention it
when bowing
shaking your petite gloved hand
after you asked about the poem
a flock of frigates flying
on the Sacrarium Steps

How did you memorise it all?
I'm a poet, Your Majesty, it's my job.
Yes, yes, I suppose it is.

Boucheron blue irises
set in the cool parchment
of your skin
lines written into Britain's history
powder-blue hat, white gloves
(changed to black in the
running of the crowd)
you are twelve sick days off
from sixty-four years of royal duty

it takes an Eckhart moment
but in those few
seconds, when we
exchange breath
we are both
Queens of the Commonwealth.

Oprah

You are the
royal 'O'
by common decree
via talk show TV
offering up the stage's platter
serving the *hors d'oeuvres* of our lives
36,000 interviews
from first black President to local resident
Yes-We-Can Obama to Ari-the-hoarder.
You share with us
at Vector Arena
that after every interview
no matter who you speak to
they all ask: *Was that ok?*
What you hear is: *Am I ok?*
You recite by memory
Caribbean king
Derek Walcott's
Love After Love.
I met him
in St Lucia
he signed my book
shook my hand

couldn't stand
because of the stroke
the day before.

In the crowd
we three lean in
kanohi ki te kanohi.

Alice Walker

Your shawl-sprawling
universe wraps
all the words
as we are pulled in
to the spinning stories
defying the gravity
of racism, sexism, history.

We are about to step
on stage at Aotea Centre
in front of a sold-out
crowd of two thousand
I ask
How would you like to walk on –
before me or after me?
You say
Let's just do this
and take my hand.
We stroll on
side by side
to a standing ovation
your hands become doves

criss-crossing above your heart
winging blessing and thanks
over fields of lavender
nodding to the wind's
womanist wisdom

welcome home Queens
welcome to yourselves.

Chapter 5

out of

one

mountain

words.

build

readily.

Dinner with the King

(for Tui Atua Tupua Tamasese Tupuola Ta'isi Efi)

Crab soup broth
Coriander, lemon grass,
Clear as the conversation between us
You ask
What's happening with our people in New Zealand?

Oka is announced
In a crystalline voice
From you, the choice of my people
Cool sliced cubes of fish
Flesh speckled with salt, lemon juice
Swim in onions, a splash of coconut cream
Raw as Nelson's hunger for Independence
As bitter lemon sweet as Tamasese's peaceful
Call for freedom
At Tuaefu
We marinate in history's juices.

Mains come
Sunset slab of salmon
An upturned cup of rice topped with curry
Green salad laced with peelings of papaya
You speak of desire for balance
Mau Samoa whose fierce independence
Is priceless
You place small grains of rice on my plate
What's happening with our people in New Zealand?

I speak of the rising generation of gafatele
Those of many bloods
The urban resurrection of spoken
Word and song
Chanting over the many places they belong
Rooted in Aotearoa.
I speak of e-books and twitterature
Self-publication, Facebook and literature
Of Al's Prime Ministerial Award
Of Lani's storming of Amazon.com
Another place where we belong
Gathering kindle, setting fire with words
Setting fire to worlds.

Vanilla bean ice-cream atolls
Rise from a sea of mango and pink guava
Tickling our throats
You speak of horizon-seeking
And of ways before papalagi, sky breakers
Met us, earth dwellers
We watch Tusi Tamasese's
O le Tulafale, a Samoan pacing
Lush silence, verdant Va
The space between us beautified.

Pinot noir and coffee
We drink in Seamus Heaney
Inhale Il Divo and Viktor Frankl's
Search for Meaning
Afters before us.

Whispers and Vanities

Whispers vanities praise profanities pre-colonial roots post-colonial off-shoots circling samoa's
head of state authors numbering 38 theologians sociologists historians
psychologists educators debaters cultural
narrators and, of course
the poets!

O le ao o le malo a song a stanza a verse each decade poetry lines traverse the indigenous
reference samoa's mythic histories our holistic connection va inviolate
mysteries binding us all to the cosmos divine
tagata land sky sea
bloodline.

Hear the rhythm of bones pound the bones to the beat the philosopher's meter in spiritual
retreat an ear for beauty an eye for strength wisdom's story the breadth the length
tui atua caller to malamalama passions victories losses drama a hand
planting ola's earth kissed trees sunlit instinct ga'au growing
free the forest's encircled stones subverting
they are tagata they are whisperers
they are vanities
flirting.

burning   hands.

Draw

no visible marks

ing   was reflected there.   as if   whole mean-

Inwood Hill, New York

(for Dåkot-ta)

For 60 guilders
Peter Minuit
For whole the sum of it
Bought Mannahatta
In 1626

That's $25 today

The whole of it
The length and breadth of it
The run of it, the line of it
The soil, rock and sag of it
The trees on it, the birds in it

But Peter Minuit
Not the people of it
Lenape, like the last tulip tree
All 280 years of it
Disappeared

Like stories
Which never quite do.

Before making

war

he   swal-
lowed

the living darkness of

Pouliuli.

97

Insurance Broker-Turned-Counsellor-Playwright, Rumba Café

There's this weedy guy in a homeless shelter
who steals these sneakers – red sneakers –
from the guy in the next bunk
big guy – you wouldn't want to mess with him –
see, before big guy sleeps
he sticks a sneaker
under a bunk leg
then one night
when the snoring starts
weedy guy crawls
under big guy's bunk
then on his back, knees to chin
with his eyes on the prize
glowing like them burning embers
in Ellsworth Park, you know
in them steel barrels

weedy guy tilts the bunk
off the floor
metal, springs
300-pound sleeping
body rises.

Later, big guy breaks
down the restroom door
finds a red-footed penguin
on the last slab of ice
nothing, Ms Poet
is ever black and white
then
LIGHTS OUT.

What do you think?

I like it very much Abraham. Cliff-hanger ending.

Yep. I want to show it at the Centre.

Oh?

Yes Ma'am. It wasn't just what you saw that day. It was all the rest.
Businesses that went bust. Families that went bust. My neighbour,
fire-fighter, he was there. Six hours at Ground Zero. Found an air
pocket. Never the same. He's there but not there – if you get my drift.
That's what the Centre's for.

I'd finished my huevos, bistec, and papas fritas
He, his maduros and red pickled onions
This one's on me – no, please.
He paid for my first meal in Union City
You never know when I might get to Nuuu Zealand.
You never know, Abraham, Father of the Nation.

When

others

glare

let the radio buzz
to an imaginary

tune.

Subway Lingo from 190th to 42nd Street

Don't be a pole hog
Keep the sound down

It's a subway not a dining car
Keep your stuff to yourself

Clipping? Primping?
It's a subway car, not a restroom

Poles are for your safety
not your latest routine

Dude . . . stop the spread, please
it's a space issue

Don't be a butt pole
please grasp poles between hands, not butt cheeks

Always offer your seat to a pregnant woman
unless she's wearing a Red Sox hat

Sicilian-Hungarian-Jersey-born Tape-Artist, Union City

My first Airbnb host is Eric
he's sleep deprived, fretful, raw
been up all night in a London cab
hailing down his next big score.

Eric wraps small items:
pens, forks, torches, vases
Ninja Turtles, Barbie and Ken dolls
Barbie and Ken cars and houses

big items: a five-metre kazoo
a statue of Lady Liberty
life-size London black cabs
parked in the lounge for free

wrapped, taped, gummed
in chequered reds, whites, blues
Marilyn Monroe splayed over the doorway
a six-foot neon Number Two

Eric exhibits in his warehouse/storage unit
accommodation/art gallery
the glorious, the magnificent
the perilous Chocolate Factory.

On his phone Eric shows me
fights with the landlord
Eric: *Just believe in me, John, believe in the art*
you believed in my work before!

John: *Eric* (counting on his fingers)
February, March, April, May
next week I bring police
I want my $19K!

Eric: *You're blind, John, blind!*
Last week I gave you a hundy
John: *Next week Eric – it's not about art*
It's about the fuckin' rent money!

John is filmed storming off
tugging between Marilyn's legs
the steel bolt finally slides through
he's Exiting out, seeing red.

But Eric's got another plan
earth shattering, untamed
with projected income from art sales
he'll invest in domain names.

He asked for my feedback:

Tapeartist.com   *predictable*
Tapevelcro.com   *semi-attachable*
Lordofthetapes.com   *maniacal*
Iwannasmuch.com   *desirable*
Ivtapedskin2.com   *unhygienic*
Igraffitiartist.com   *think I've seen it*
Humanhaircoat.com   *wax lyrical*
Hiphoproulette.com   *Redfoo miracle*
Friedcannolis.com   *Sicilian roots*
Faceyourflow.com   *New Age off shoot*
Exitthroughthetapeshop.com   *hope it brings in money*
Tapeartisttape.com   *just not that funny*

Steam from Eric's e-cigarette
fingers his rusty afro
as he rocks in the bamboo swing-seat
slung from kitchen catapult gizmo

he won't go partying tonight
it ruins art-making for days
he'll stay tight with his inventions
they keep Willy Wonka unfazed.

The *New York Times*, April 21 2015

A2

At a news conference on monday death trying to balance responsibilities underscored a new realisation find diverse allies in new york and reassure journalism's intimate obsessions.

B2

The dead convene to plan a new approach to bodies sinking in illicit ideology history will judge its stories in other words visits to the mall embezzle saliva instead of blood.

C2

I understand everything better especially now that searing valleys of technology tumble in the music into the dark touching the void unfriended.

D2

Humans lie unguarded in the sacredness of a day temples protest suffering and sceptical questions but faith has been with us for three days in tents unguarded a riot of archetypal stars near a homeless shelter revive death.

the story.

began to massage

his painful

errors

like the   tail of a stingray.

45

Eviction Notice 113

her house has become a party her house has become a body her house has become a party her house has become a body her house has become a party her house has become a body her house has become a party her house has become a body her house has become a party her house has become become become become become become be calm be calm be calm be calm be calm the house has become mum the house has become mum the house has become mum the house has become mum the house has become mum the house has become become become become become becalm becalm be calm be calm become a body become a party become a body become a party become a body become a party become a body become a party become a body become a party become a

body party body party body party body party body party body party body party body party body party body party body party body party body party body a part body a part body a part body a part body a part body a part body a part body a part body a part body a part body a part body a part body a part her body's become a part her body's become a part her body's become a part her body's become a part her body's become a part her body's become a part her body's become a part her body's become a body apart her body's become a body a part her body's become a body apart her body's become a body a part her body's become a body apart her body's become a body a part party party party party party party party party t t t t t t t t t t t t t t t t t t t t t

her house has become a body a part her house has become a body a part her house has become a body a part her house has become a body a part her house has become a body a part her house has become her house has become her house has become her house has become her house has become her house has become ours has become her house ours has become her house her house has become ours her house has become ours her house has become ours ours has become hours ours has become hours her house has become her body apart ours has become her body apart house has become her body apart

63

ours has become her body apart ours has become ours has become ours has become be calm be calm be calm body party body party body party body party body party t t t t t t t t t t body party body party body party t t t t t t t t t a body a part a body a part a body a part a body a part a body a part a body a body a part a body a part a body a part a body a part a body a part a body body depart body depart body depart body depart body depart body depart body depart body depart body depart body depart body depart body depart ours has become a body apart ours has become a body apart ours has become a body apart ours has become a body apart ours has become a body apart t t t t t t t

Essential Oils for the Dying

Take this cardamom
to ease you into the next plane
not the one taking you back to Santa Cruz
or Honolulu or Suva
but the next plane.

Wrap frankincense round
your bones for warm acceptance
of why the good and the young

ginger will raise its hand
palm side out
to the rabid dog
its wounded mouth

grapefruit will secd
inner peace and green saplings
of forgiveness.

If you're terrified of dying, if it
at every moment, tightens its grip round
your bleeding pancreas
its clustering bombs
lemon is there.

I will not give you myrrh
for the long, slow dying.

I will not give you ylang ylang
to bring you to yourself
everyone knows you Tere
you've always known your self

your grace-filled voice
truth and anger in mixed parts
lolomas and alofaz in mixed parts.

I remember your coconut-oil voice
immiscible with injustice –
my first academic conference
your paper on Ocean Island mining
the holes, the drilling
the image on the screen
ashen crevices deep
Bwanaba's cracked leeched earth
open sores weeping dust –
your coconut-oil voice, a gentle thrum
so everyone had to lean in

then the edge of it broke
as you spoke, the camera pulled away
Bwanaba's barren and broken land
became the back of your grandfather's hand –
from land mines to land lines to life lines
his wrinkled skin
the world held within his palm.

So no ylang ylang for you
dear one

but for the rest of us
cypress for sorrow
chamomile for resentment, tension
and bitter-sweet melissa
to press against the loss.

Bread Bags

The pole house
shades the woman
straightening furled
strands of pandanus
pulling knuckle-tight
plaiting into submission
for the kula
– a chief, like the tide, will rise.

Yesterday she used
the same technique
to weave hats from cut and stripped
Tip Top bread bags
waterproof panamas, boaters, bowlers, fedoras
in road-cone orange
sunflower yellow, Frigidaire white.

There are no sunflowers in Tuvalu
but plenty of road cones
pimple Funafuti's eroded coral-packed paths
plenty of Frigidaires
rust off their hinges
in borrow pits.

Tomorrow she will weave more hats.

Te Moana-nui-a-Kiwa
fusses at floorboards
whacking the mat
she shuffles back
to higher ground.

Atoll Haiku Chain

Mururoa, isle
atoll of the Great Secret
prophetically named

by Ma'ohi tongues
before French nuclear arms
tests in '66

then in '95
tear gas, guns, makeshift weapons
Tahiti's streets burned

palm trees, buildings flamed
chains, rocks, hurtled in protest
as mushroom clouds rise.

Tahiti, islands
of native secrets, no more
than when Wallis's

cannons burned waters
1767
imperial right.

2002
Ma'ohi words fire and flame
Varua Tupu.

alofa

The only trustworthy

promised

Nadadola Road

We climb in on Semo Road
Nadi to Suva
185 kilometres.
Erin from Boston, Jo from London, me
Mr Indo-Fiji-Taxi-Driver-Man
stops after ten minutes
for the wild, syrupy flesh
of $5 a bowl green mangoes.
We cut a swathe, at 110 ks
through gravel road
fair-haired sugarcane fields
jaded hills, houses on stilts
Viaviani Beach's heat-faded sign.

We plea-pray for official passing lanes
as Mr Indo-Fiji-Taxi-Driver-Man
picks his nose at a leisurely pace
investigates the gravel gathered there.
Carpenters Hardware's flat-bed truck
slows us down, we watch the
squat concrete blocks wobble on board
unsecured. We watch the top row
lean away from the corner
as we fly past market stalls of pumpkins
purple gobi cabbage, cauliflower.

Mr Indo-Fiji-Taxi-Driver-Man
bumper kisses the flat-bed
sparking the island dialect
of horn-speak and wound down window

sign language
with two fingers splitting the air
Mr Indo-Fiji-Taxi-Driver-Man
yells *Get off road! You too slow!*
while texting and overtaking
round the corner
indicators, a sign of weakness.

If Erin could see what I could see
she'd kill him and then me
for not saving our lives
for not saying with Bostonian surety
Sir, put that god-damn phone away!
I keep thinking it'll be a short txt
who am I to impose my foreign ways?

Sigatoka's sand hills carve out billboard landscapes
Fish n Trips: Game Fishing
Breadwinner Dead: Over Speeding
Korotogo: 122 kms

Mr Indo-Fiji-Taxi-Driver-Man
sucks salty peas
then licking his herb-crested fingertips
digs into the packet
and holds some out to share.

Apia Seawall

drain in
drain out

drain rain	ocean din
drain spout	floating log
drain drum	rusted tin
drain strain	float up
string strung	back in
pop rain	tide rise
pop stop	short fin
rock wind	current pull
slur spin	tack wind
shoot turn	stacked pack
shout bin	pop pin
beach fin	salt sea
face front	surge in
back in	drain rain
island drain	hop slop
scoop sloop	sea in
tongue flute	sea talk
land rain	sea song
tide strain	drain throat
island sin	steel long
	ocean swill
	salt spout

drain in
drain out

the

Genesis

of the world.

is

a

tongue in
rain

Path

The ala
is a bridge
a road

a dog walking
the dust-eating Taiwan earth
is a tuna flying

through the sea's
salt and spit
is a tongue

a voice
the wind, sun and stars
is a telling

a tale
is what is told
what will be told

what is untold
is an Amis shaman
a Calai

a circling of hands
over heaped ginger roots
is an invisible thread

a long metal spike pinpointing
the path of restitution.
The ala

is a showing of hands
and feet
a line of three

a row of banana leaves
waving forth the dead
is a pile of basil

and sticky rice pancakes
an invitation back
in orange and white

is a root
a route
a vein

a hanging bridge
is a super freeway
between East and West

is a landfall of islands in-between
is a hunting trail
scented by stories

of settlement trails
is a funeral song
bringing you home.

III

trick

believe

in the plot.
you form
in secrecy

All you have to worry about is

t h e

drive

133

The Working Mother's Guide to Reading Seventy Books a Year

Don't have the babies

Don't have a full-time job

Don't be working class

Don't be time poor and extended family rich

If you did have the babies, don't let them play sports
Definitely don't let them play an instrument
(extramural activities increase peak-hour traffic commuting time)

Have a partner, but only if they don't mind not seeing you
Definitely put a bookshelf in Nana's room to handle the overflow –
of washing, not books
If you did need that full-time job, put your foot down and don't work past 5pm
Don't need much sleep

If you are working class, do read about all the reading working-class people do.
Like Jeanette Winterson who hid 77 paperbacks under her ever-rising single-
bed mattress until her torch-bearing mother spied an overhanging leaf, which
turned into a branch, which turned into a tree laden with leaves and leaves
and leaves, which mother, doing God's gardening, pulled up by the roots,
dragged into the midnight yard and lit.

A bonfire of words and ords and rds and ds and sss

As the smoke stung her eyes
Jeanette inhaled its burning kiss
Vowing to commit the stories to memory

Then vowed one better:
I'll write my own.

Read at half time when the water-boy runs on the field skipping
Read one-handed in line at Countdown while lifting
Read in the car waiting for the coach to finish his speech on quitting
Read in the kitchen while the crockpot's stewing
Read on the handbagged Kindle while it's charging

Read knowing it's not a competition
Read poetry, read creative non-fiction
Even if it takes you the whole year, read a novel.

be afraid of

nothing and nobody
b
a

slave

to

love.

115

Like the Time You Were Four

I was in London
chiming a rhyme at the foot of Big Ben
you first told the time
when the face of the clock
was the backdrop
you said 'tick tock, mummy o'clock'
and I thought
time to get home.

Like the time you were seven
I was in Paris
cobbling words together from the
Saint-Étienne-du-Mont
dark, damp etchings
on my screen you came up like the sun
salty glint of Waiheke sea spray
I missed your shape among the stone and the clay.

Like the time you were twelve
I was in New York
plugging into the page
flashing Times Square syllables
you were learning your eight times tables
we calculated the sleeps until
I'd get home
you were alone, under the covers
with your iPod
Nana and Dad thought you were sleeping
but you and me were dreaming.

Like the time you were sixteen
I was in St Lucia
building a metaphor from Walcott's *White Egrets*
I kept reading *White Regrets*.
Facetime wasn't working
but you and me were msging
in real time
about the try line, your scoring, that missed tackle
and in the heat
I missed you and your Auckland winter.

Like the time you were twenty-three
thirty-eight
forty-four
fifty-one
sixty
and I am not there, but there
and we are facetiming.

Orange Crayon Stick Figure Man

(on the occasion of reading 'with' Sam Hunt at the Parnell Rose
Gardens, only to discover that 'with' was employed euphemistically to
describe sharing the same venue, but performing at different times)

Sam, Sam
my orange crayon stick figure man
I love you
because you are what you do
and did what you said
back in '82
I was eleven when you came
to our Avondale school
you looked drunk
but you were nobody's fool
like the unsung pied piper
you played your own tune

and we followed
and we followed

in shirt hung like a rolling stone maxim
flung over black exclamation mark jeans
puncturing our *poetry rulz 4eva*
and I loved you

and we followed
and we followed

and we followed
your DB Draught words
your hill rolling slurs

your breaths your chants your lamentations
your strides your quivers your gesticulations

so, I wanna beg your pardon
I know you never promised me a rose garden
but here we are
and I'm doing what you did
and I'm telling

Sam, Sam
my orange crayon stick figure man
we'd only just begun
when you coloured in my tongue
waxing oh so lyrical, tragical, comical
Kiwi Shakespeare shearing in our school hall
from one rant to the next
to the other and the one after that and that

Sam
you one cool cat
and
I love you.

Marriage

Ring

Don't aim only to dodge
your sparring partner's weapons
don't remain only on the defensive

Use your opponent's tactics
to cultivate speed and familiarity
to counter attack

Footwork is important
don't move without purpose, reason
or utility

Watch your opponent's feet
when entering the ring

Never open your mouth or bite your lip
if you do
you will be injured if hit
causing unnecessary pain

Try to rid yourself
of this kind of habit.

Vows

Note: Each camp has its own way
But one thing should be borne in mind
Never use plaster or scotch tape
Around the knuckles
This would make a hard and lethal edge
Such would not be fair
It would not be a sport or an art or a skill
It would be murder

Naked fist or rope-bound fist
Raw cotton or piece of string
Raw cotton hardens
With sweat
Becomes sandpaper
Causes cuts and lacerations
This method was abandoned
When a fighter died
Soft cotton bandages
Of not more than 2.5 metres in length
Are used now.

Anniversary

All the world's animals struggle
Lowest to highest
Struggle to be born
Struggle in death

A Thai boxer knows
He must rely
On someone more
Knowledgeable
More experienced
Than he

To teach
The art
The science
The philosophy
Of training

Where art
Is above force.

Belief in Jack Kerouac

he told me
woman, never get drunk
outside your own house

find love in form
with crazy dumb saints
maybe, this one

I blew deep
from his unspeakable visions
he scribbled notebooks

it was his wild joy
his words were everything
open and listening

he told me his poetry
had visionary tics
transfixed, I began to scratch

my left shoulder
come closer, he said
and share my interior monologue

I think I'm in love
with your jewel centre
your eye within your eye

you have a pithy middle, I said
it languages the sea
only because I accept loss forever, he said

you have holy contours, I replied
but not for me
their struggle-worlds flow

I need to know how to stop
to see this picture better
in the mooning light

you're right, he said
I write exact pictures
I'm a book-movie

playing a bleak, inhuman loneliness
its sequel of stormed
undisciplined pure

and you woman
are sponsored in heaven

lies sometimes

cure

poetical exhortations

forsake.

forgiveness.

Red Comb

(for Lonnie)

ruby-red steel comb
tip-toeing on its teeth

flowering blooming arseholes
black pearl reddening

laughing in relief
captive nature

turns provocateur
in white spaces-in-between

Black White Desiring

After all the

Post Colonial Theory	Imperial Geo-Political	Black Skin / White Mask
Oceanic Literary Study	Cartography	Psychology
Pacific Epistemology	Capitalist Topography	Margin / Centre Ontology
Global Indigenous Research	Racist Iconography	Ethno-Poetic Ethnography
Methodology	Sexist Typography	MLA or APA Bibliography

I watch *The Vampire Diaries*

blood sucking,	fang-bangers,	re-wiring
triangulating tyrannies	wolf-jammers conspiring	after a year of
love-lorn, love-lust diarising	scholarly and pop culture	territorial indigenising

it's all just a transfusion of desiring

In Creative Writing Class

the pākehā man
calls the kailoma Fijian woman
the Māori woman
and the ʻafakasi Samoan woman
privileged
because they have the experience
of being doubly oppressed
at a time when they qualify
for certain scholarships
when their demographic
is fashionable and interesting
their life experiences
make their writing more convincing
their stories are rich and deep
hot chocolatey and steamy
his are staid, North Shore-ish
lukewarmish gumboot tea

the los atrevido
wait for him to finish
his first world problems
in their global village
their serpent tongues aim
for the space above his collar
they fire simultaneously
no one even hears him holler

Warrior Poetry

Putting together a poetry collection, boys
is like the NRL Nines
Eden Park, 45,000 packed
you've got 90 pages of lines
to work the eclectic crowd
into some kinda synthesis – some kinda wonderful

but your poems are

Len Brown twins, arm in arm
yokelling up the stairs
Fred Flintstone and Wilma, jiving
in fluffy pig's feet and ears

vikings thundering with axes
tiny elves digging the seats
their spades are used to ward off
purple flower-potted peeps

but your poems are

tigers slapping their tails
over Shirley Temple's moko
doctors in white coats stethoscope-shouting
Everybody's loco!

rabbit heads on lime lettuce beds
sipping carb zero sav blanc
thinking boldly, treading lightly
but always spilling the plonk

cavemen with mismatching beards
but strangely matching socks
they club the French barmaids in black 'n' white
whose hairy chests cause shocks

(under tutus French suspenders
should always be kept out of sight
it's obvious *that* poem's been round the block –
a poem of the night)

but your poems are

shimmering pharaohs, smiling-sombreroed
ukulele-strumming Mexicans
turquoise-caped commandoes, X-men bravados
guarded by Roman centurions

they are Batmen, jesters, jailers, Uncle Festers
beach babes wearing tuxedos
they herd round the two-person brown cow
where ever the front goes the back goes

they are pirates swinging swords slashing the hordes
crowded round bare-breasted mermaids
Where's Wally keeps looking, high and low searching
for the contrabanding French barmaids

Mary Poppins flirts, loses his skirt
now looks like a K-Road gigolo
he lands next to Bif, who thrives on a whiff
of moustacheod fame from *The Footy Show*

and when your poems are

cat calls, crowd-surfing balls
and transparent floating condoms
foaming hands, portable bandstands
and flying Chitty Chitty Bang Bangs

Aloha shirts and leis perverted
on brawny browned muscle men
loose blond hair flicking everywhere
hiding the rum and semen

dwarves riding astride blown-up
dragons wearing Rastafarian wigs
black-silver Warriors selfie preening
smooching the life-size lipsticks

and when your poems are

transformers policing
while cracking a Woody
gangsters throwing shade
from under black hoodies

zumba dancing bananas
front peels hanging down
exposé fruit
signed by all around

then you know, boys
putting together a poetry collection
means synching this kinda crowd
where flicking the page
like a Mexican wave
has gotta leave the reader wowed.

never

wound a

new

bird-

21

Ka'ena, Leaping Point

('Oahu, Hawai'i)

Albatross toss about
in the wind above
my head

they play with air currents
I play with myth
their chicks

not yet mobile
flick flecked beaks
up and down

near the round
monk seals
slabs of silver velveteen

sunning, nearby yellow
faced bees
ease into low-lying

salmon-coloured 'ohai
beyond salty mists
whales breach then burst

spouting stars in the sky
I stand on the shore's
jutting tableau tongue

I am a vowel
aaaaaaa
wide armed, open mouthed

aaaaaaaing into the Va
a breeze carries
sacred echoes back

but not mine, not yet
I am still
unleapt

Notes

Wendt quote taken from Antony Hooper et al., 'Novelists and Historians and the Art of Remembering' in *Class and Culture in the South Pacific* (Suva: Institute of Pacific Studies, 78–92). These lines have been variously quoted in print and artworks. The Blackout poems are taken from the novel *Pouliuli* (first edition) by Albert Wendt (Longman Paul, 1977).

'Apostles': Marengo is a mining company in Papua New Guinea. Shirley Jackson's short story 'The Lottery' was first published in 1948 in the *New Yorker*.

'Unity': Commissioned by the Commonwealth Foundation, the poem needed to adhere to five rules: 1) it had to address the theme of inclusivity; 2) it had to appeal to a broad audience, from the thousand schoolchildren gathered from across the UK, to heads of state, various dignitaries and the Royal Family; 3) it had to represent the 53 member countries of the Commonwealth; 4) it had to be under three minutes, as the BBC was filming it live; 5) it was not permitted to be political.

'Pussy Cat' has an audiovisual version available on Youtube: 'Selina Tusitala Marsh's response to Commonwealth Observance Day 2016', www.youtube.com/watch?v=fz1tx7pTB-8

'Queens I have met': The late Te Arikinui Dame Te Ātairangikaahu is Aotearoa's longest-reigning Māori monarch.

Victor Frankl's book *Man's Search for Meaning* was first published in English in 1962 by Beacon Press.

'Bread Bags': Kula, a Tuvalu headdress, often prepared for the inauguration of a chief (aliki).

'Atoll Haiku Chain': *Vārua Tupu: New Writing From French Polynesia* (*Mānoa: A Pacific Journal of International Writing*, University of Hawai'i Press, 2006) is the first major anthology of Mā'ohi writing.

Fa'afetai tele lava, Thank you

Thanks to Anna Hodge for editing early drafts, Jane Parkin for her close-up pīwakawaka's eye, and Tusiata Avia for her swoop-in soaring kererū's eye. Fa'afetai tele lava to Al and Reina for their alofa, especially to Al for allowing me to create new windows of light into his early work. Also thanks to Samantha Lelei Crosbie for her constant belief, Sivamalie Siva Forsyth for his stories, Tim Page for music and creative musings, and His Highness Tui Atua Tupua Tamasese Tupuola Ta'isi Efi for talanoa. Thanks to David . . . my ellipsis, Javan-Micah-Davey, my hyphens, and Noelle Grace, my exclamation mark!